Martha
Stewart
In Her Own Words

Martha Stewart

In Her Own Words

EDITED BY
Suzanne Sonnier

A B2 BOOK

Agate

CHICAGO

Printed in the United States of America

Martha Stewart: In Her Own Words

ISBN 13: 978-1-57284-288-5
ISBN 10: 1-57284-288-1
eISBN 13: 978-1-57284-840-5
eISBN 10: 1-57284-840-5

First printing: August 2020

10 9 8 7 6 5 4 3 2 1   20 21 22 23 24 25

Agate books are available in bulk at discount prices. For more information, go to agatepublishing.com.

I was serving a desire—not only mine, but every home-maker's desire, to elevate that job of homemaker. It was floundering, I think. And we all wanted to escape it, to get out of the house, get that high-paying job and pay somebody else to do everything that we didn't think was really worthy of our attention. And all of a sudden I realized it was terribly worthy of our attention.

—*THE NEW YORKER*, FEBRUARY 13, 2000

Contents

Introduction...1

Part I: Foundations

    Nutley Days...6

    Early Adulthood...16

    Values...27

Part II: Good Things

    Food 48

    Entertaining 59

    Decorating..70

    Gardening...76

    Animals 84

Part III: Hard Times

    Insider Trading Scandal...90

    Prison and Home Confinement.................................99

Part IV: Empire

    Business Philosophy 109

    Media...126

    Merchandising 145

Milestones.. 153

Acknowledgments 176

Introduction

Just about everyone has an opinion on Martha Stewart, America's best-known expert on homemaking and entertaining. These opinions can be remarkably strong and polarized relative to her wholesome aim of bringing "good things" to people's lives. Whatever one thinks of her, Stewart's arc of stratospheric rise, precipitous fall, and remarkable comeback is as American as a slice of her homemade pie.

Little about her ordinary upbringing suggests that great success would be in her future. Stewart was born to Polish-Catholic, working-class parents in 1941, the second of six children raised in a modest neighborhood in New Jersey. Growing up, she learned gardening lessons from her father and homemaking skills from her mother. By some accounts, her father was demanding and encouraged his daughter's perfectionist tendencies in all things.

Intelligent and hardworking, Stewart excelled in school. When she was curious about something, she learned all she could until she became proficient. This would become a hallmark of her life and career.

Her enterprise and good looks led to modeling jobs while still in high school, which continued through college at Barnard and into the early years of her marriage. Then, after her father-in-law taught her about the stock market, Stewart became a licensed broker and worked on Wall Street.

After moving with her husband and baby daughter to a historic Connecticut farmhouse, Turkey Hill, in the early 1970s, Stewart threw herself into cooking from scratch and renovating the house and grounds. Eventually she quit her Wall Street job altogether to run a catering business from her home kitchen.

Catering in her prosperous Connecticut community led to connections and a publishing deal. Her book *Entertaining*, published in 1982, became a bestseller and launched a media empire. Stewart described the areas of her expertise as "living," which included but was not limited to cooking, baking, entertaining, decorating, gardening, crafting, and homemaking—all treated with her trademark elegance. She soon became known as a master of the domestic arts. As Stewart put it, "I was trying to make a business out of lifestyle. No one had ever done that before. So I was a pioneer in trying to make lifestyle an actual business. And I think I succeeded rather well." By any metric, Stewart is correct.

Her success was built on her image as a polished and patient mentor who could make routine tasks into interesting, even glamorous endeavors. She did this first through her books, and then via television, a magazine, radio, social media, design, and product licensing. As the go-to expert in the profession she'd invented, she grew an eponymous empire, employing hundreds of people to expand her brand and support her vision. And she became a cultural phenomenon.

Stewart was more than a lifestyle doyenne, though. She proved to be an exceptionally sharp businessperson as well. In 1997, she had the foresight to buy all of her publishing, television, and retail operations, which she merged to create the company Martha Stewart Living Omnimedia. The initial public offering of MSLO stock two years later made Stewart the first self-made female billionaire in the United States.

She also disrupted stereotypical gender roles. While her subject matter focused on the traditionally female domain of the comforts of home, she was unapologetically competitive and ambitious in business. In combining the two spheres of homemaking and business, Stewart shattered the limits of narrow gender stereotypes.

But not everyone was an admirer. As her public profile grew, critics accused Stewart of being an untrained dilettante, overconfident and didactic. The media mocked her as cold and out of touch. While legions of fans emulated Stewart, a growing chorus of fault-finders ridiculed her.

Ill will toward Stewart reached a crescendo with the ImClone scandal of the early 2000s, in which she was investigated for insider trading, obstruction of justice, and conspiracy related to her sale of 4,000 shares of ImClone Systems stock. Stewart, usually as perfectly composed as her exquisite trays of hors d'oeuvres, was rattled by the SEC investigation, subsequent trial, public scorn, and made-for-TV movies that resulted. Though she unflaggingly proclaimed her innocence and believed she was unfairly being made an example, she was convicted of lying to the government, obstruction of justice, and conspiracy. She was not convicted of securities fraud; essentially, she was found guilty of a cover-up.

Stewart served a five-month prison term at

Alderson Federal Prison Camp in rural West Virginia. The women-only, minimum-security facility was nicknamed "Camp Cupcake" by the media for its relative luxury, but Stewart found her prison experience "horrifying." Home confinement for five months and probation followed her sentence.

Once past the nadir, her comeback was swift. Having lost her Emmy-winning show *Martha Stewart Living* during her legal troubles, she soon bounced back with a satellite radio channel, a TV talk show, and a spinoff of *The Apprentice*. Inspired by the frequent advice-seeking of her fellow prison inmates, Stewart wrote a new bestseller, *The Martha Rules*, on how to start and run a successful business. She resumed making media and licensing deals and writing more bestselling books. She also founded the Martha Stewart Center for Living at Mount Sinai Medical Center, focusing on the health care needs of older adults. In 2015, Stewart sold MSLO to Sequential Brands for $355 million. Sequential sold the business to Marquee Brands, at a steep loss, in 2019. Stewart remains involved with the company.

Today, Stewart is not only back, she is everywhere. Fans can find her on magazine stands, bookstores, radio, retail outlets, and television. Her unlikely TV pairing with rapper Snoop Dogg and stints on celebrity roasts on Comedy Central have boosted Stewart's reputation and yielded an entirely new audience.

Martha Stewart's story is both original and quintessentially American. The self-made business titan took her lumps and emerged victorious, implacable, and ready to resume teaching us all a thing or two.

Part I

FOUNDATIONS

Nutley Days

I learned so much from my mother. She taught me about the importance of home and history, family and tradition.

—*Living the Good Long Life: A Practical Guide to Caring for Yourself and Others*, April 23, 2013

MY MOM, SHE was a very good example to me of wanting to elevate a simple life into a really good life.

—*Next Question with Katie Couric* podcast, October 5, 2017

MOM KNEW HOW to feed a large group with a minimum of fuss and waste, with an emphasis on wholesome foods, simply prepared. We never ate so-called convenience foods.

—*Everyday Food: Great Food Fast*, March 13, 2017

MY MOM, BIG Martha … was a fabulous preserver, following the traditions established by her immigrant mother, Yadviga Ruskowski. Mom made garlic dills and sour dills and soft dills and crispy dills, all in six to eight gallon earthenware glazed crocks.

—*The Martha Blog*, August 28, 2015

MY MOTHER OBVIOUSLY was not too concerned with my dexterity since she gave me, from a very early age, complete freedom in her kitchen in our home in Nutley. It was nice to be trusted, and it encouraged me to experiment and create freely.

—MarthaStewart.com, December 22, 2014

I DEVELOPED A love for lavender as a small girl. My father grew it in his very sunny garden in Nutley, New Jersey.

—*The Martha Blog*, September 11, 2009

Cooking was
a huge part of
Mom's life and
she loved sharing
her recipes. The
recipes I learned
from her are
among our most
requested
year after year.

—*The Martha Blog,* May 4, 2019

MY FONDNESS FOR currants goes right back to my childhood when I would carefully harvest the jewel-like berries from the bushes that my father planted in one corner of our large back yard. Later, in the kitchen, after carefully removing the stems, I would assist my mother, who always put up jars and jars of delicious, clear, ruby red jelly.

—*The Martha Blog*, July 13, 2008

I WAS THE only one of my father's children who took naturally to the garden—I never minded the hours in the blazing sun, weeding and cultivating. My father sent for every garden catalogue available, and we pored over them together, choosing what we would like to have on an imaginary estate, as well as what we could actually afford to have and take care of.

—*New York* Magazine, June 26, 2008

I CLEARLY REMEMBER my maternal grandmother's sun porch on Huntington Avenue in Buffalo, New York, where she puttered daily, caring for her large assortment of houseplants—deadheading spent blooms, cutting away withered leaves, and shaping leggy specimens into more manageable forms.

—**MarthaStewart.com, c. 2018**

WHEN I WAS growing up, in a middle-class family of eight in Nutley, New Jersey, Christmas was our most intensely celebrated holiday. We baked, we cooked, we decorated with boughs and artificial snow. We always stayed at home, surrounded by our family, lots of relatives, many friends, and modest gifts.

—**MarthaStewart.com, December 22, 2014**

MAKING GIFTS TO give, rather than buying gifts for our numerous relatives and friends, was always the preference in our family. The boys would be busy in the basement workroom, where Dad kept his tools, jigsawing or carving or whittling or gluing. The girls would be in the kitchen, at the table or at the counters, mixing doughs to exact measurements, chopping candied fruits, cracking nuts and extracting the meat from the shells, or stirring icings and decorating finished baked goods.

—MarthaStewart.com, December 22, 2014

I WAS A crafter and artist as a child, always looking for a project that would result in something special to give to Mom, take to school, or display in our home.

—*Martha Stewart's Favorite Crafts for Kids*, June 18, 2013

I READ MANY books a week and was rewarded
by my parents, but only if I also accomplished
all of my chores—gardening, sewing, and ironing
... My interest in anything and everything home
oriented developed—and I read about design and
decoration and developed good taste in all things
domestic.

**—YMA Fashion Scholarship Fund's Annual Awards Gala
speech, January 10, 2019**

I HAD A reading chair that I sat in and read in. I
also had a favorite tree that I sat in and read in.
It sounds a little idyllic, you know, sort of Mark
Twain-ish, but it was true.

—interview, Academy of Achievement, June 2, 1995

THE MOST IMPORTANT lesson I learned from my parents was drilled into my head on a regular basis: "Work hard, try hard, and most of your goals will be realized. Don't limit yourself." This advice not only helped me develop a sense of self-worth and self-confidence, but also reinforced my belief that excellence could be achieved in many endeavors.

—MarthaStewart.com, December 19, 2014

IF YOU DON'T work hard, it's all for naught. My mother's favorite word: naught. N-A-U-G-H-T. I hear that in my head every single day.

—commencement address at The Culinary Institute of America, April 15, 2011

MY FATHER ALSO used to tell me, "Remember, Martha, girls can do anything. Anything." This was in the 1950s—not exactly the most progressive time in America. But that is what he would say: Girls can do anything. And I believed him, and I still do.

—speech at NYWIFT Muse Awards, 2011

PEOPLE ARE LIKE, "Oh, my God, you know everything!" I don't know so much—other people just know so little. I know pretty much what my generation learned because we had home economics, we had cooking classes in school.

—*Parents,* 2013

I WAS THE girl next door. I was the girl that all parents held up as the example to their daughters, "Why can't you be like Martha?"

—interview, Academy of Achievement, June 2, 1995

I DO WHAT I please, and I do it with ease.

—yearbook declaration, Nutley High School yearbook, 1959

Early Adulthood

WELL, IF TRUTH be told, I wanted to go to
Stanford. But that was California. I had never
been to California, I had only seen pictures of
California. It was, to me, a romantic place. I
don't mean romantic romantic, but I meant, "Oh,
my gosh, it's exotic." It's far away from home, it
would totally free me from my family, but my
family was having problems, financial problems,
at the time. I felt very obligated to stay around,
contribute.

—interview, Academy of Achievement, June 2, 1995

I WAS A model all during high school. That paid
for college. And all during college.

—*Today*, October 3, 2018

MODELING GAVE ME a sense of self-confidence in
front of the camera, which I've used, and am still
using it, every single day.

—*Skimm'd from the Couch* podcast, December 5, 2018

MODELING WAS A wonderful way to supplement our family's income, but I wanted to build a career. I longed to do something more intellectually stimulating.

—*The Martha Rules*, October 11, 2005

MY FATHER-IN-LAW WAS a stockbroker, and I had been investing our savings on Wall Street with him. And I learned about companies, and I learned about business, and it was very intriguing. So when I was ready to look for a real full-time job upon graduation from college, I decided that that would be kind of an interesting career path.

—*Skimm'd from the Couch* podcast, December 5, 2018

AFTER COLLEGE I got a job on Wall Street, where I became an institutional stockbroker. The job taught me so much about what it takes to build a real business, a real company—a meaningful and useful enterprise. Yet it was not until I left Wall Street that I discovered my true entrepreneurial bent. I loved ideas. I loved building. I loved creating. I loved making things that would enhance everyday living. And I loved making money as a result.

—**MarthaStewart.com, 2017**

I JUST LEARNED a lot about business as a broker. And it was a very interesting job with a very interesting group of characters.

—*Skimm'd from the Couch* **podcast, December 5, 2018**

WE HAD A penthouse, on the 21st floor, for a few months. It was pretty classy for a little girl from Nutley, New Jersey! It was quite extraordinary to be so high, with a wraparound terrace; plus it was built as a luxury East Side co-op. I think it was $125 a month.

—*New York* **Magazine, November 21, 2018**

I ENTERTAINED ALL the time, and I had a penchant for decorating. We bought an old wreck of a house called Turkey Hill, and that started the career in homemaking. And all this was while I was commuting being a stockbroker.

—on her first home renovation project, of a 1805 schoolhouse, *Skimm'd from the Couch* **podcast, December 5, 2018**

TURKEY HILL WAS my original farmhouse and my first 'laboratory', where my 'empire' began. It's been featured in my magazines and on my television shows. I would not be who I am today without the vast knowledge I gained at Turkey Hill.

—*The Martha Blog*, June 5, 2017

[THE TURKEY HILL] house, on a tract of land that stretched south toward Long Island Sound and had once been an onion farm, came with two acres of deep, loamy soil, a few large trees, and not much else. There was no garage or barn, just a rickety picket fence and an unkempt yard. . . . There was not much of a kitchen and no usable bathroom. The basement was damp, and there was no porch, terrace, garden, or driveway. But it had good bones, lovely windows, wide-plank floors, and seven fireplaces. To us, it was perfect: a do-it-yourself project resplendent with opportunity.

—MarthaStewart.com, September 20, 2018

IT HAD NO indoor plumbing and rudimentary electricity so I really learned how to do everything from simple painting and spackling, to brick laying, to carpentry (I made the kitchen cabinets), to electrical wiring and laying pipe for plumbing.

—*The Martha Blog*, September 15, 2009

ALMOST EVERY GARDENING experiment was successful. Transplanted trees always took root, and once established, the beeches and fruit trees and magnolias grew magnificently. It seemed there was always a gentle breeze, with no bugs, no pests, and no need for air-conditioning. Even the animals, domesticated or not, coexisted very well.

—MarthaStewart.com, September 20, 2018

TURKEY HILL WAS a dream place for my family and me for many years. It taught us, it nurtured us, it fed us, and it occupied us in so many wonderful and instructive ways. I would not be who I am today without the vast knowledge I gained there, on that small bit of paradise.

—MarthaStewart.com, September 20, 2018

FAST-GROWING COMPANIES ALL started off with a really good idea. That's where I got the idea that I could do something in the field that I was most interested in, which was homemaking . . . So I started a catering business.

—*Seventeen*, October 22, 2006

CATERING PAVED THE way for me to find my true passion as a teacher and a communicator of Good Things.

—*The Martha Rules*, October 11, 2005

THAT CAME IN about 1979 when I realized that the work I was doing, which was original and creative, the preparation of food, the serving of food, the building of a business from a basement, it was just the time when women were finally thinking, oh boy, we better get back to work. I agreed. I agreed that we could—but I agreed, and I thought, that we could probably do it from home.

—interview, Academy of Achievement, June 2, 1995

I WORKED INCREDIBLY hard to set myself apart from other caterers. My parties had to look different, they had to taste different, and they had to deliver an altogether different experience than those of other caterers. Nothing was too much effort.

—*The Martha Rules*, October 11, 2005

I HAD TO fight town regulations and rules and laws, I had to persuade the health departments that I could cook from my home, I had very difficult neighbor problems, and yet I was sort of paving the way for a lot of women to go back to work. And it was very interesting. I could have done it very differently. I could have just left my house and gone to a catering kitchen somewhere and spent all my days there—12, 15, 20 hours a day somewhere else. But because I stayed at home, because I still went out and picked the vegetables from my garden and gathered the eggs from my chickens and used all those things and the flowering roses and the lilies and everything from my garden, I created a style that I couldn't have done if I hadn't been organically interested in what was going on around me. And that is what gave me my edge, and gave me the opportunity to realize that what I was doing was art.

—interview, Academy of Achievement, June 2, 1995

I HAD ASKED my husband to preheat the oven to 300 degrees. He had just put it on broil. So we woke up to a house full of black smoke. The turkey was totally charred on the outside. And this was at 7:00 a.m. And I started to cry. And I got in the car, I jumped in the car—my husband thought I was leaving him. I should have then. It would have been better. No, I'm just kidding!

—on her first/worst Thanksgiving ever, Talks at Google, November 6, 2011

I COULD'VE MARRIED the next guy, or the next guy, but I didn't. I'm not unhappy about that.

—*Next Question with Katie Couric* podcast, October 5, 2017

Values

ONCE YOU REALIZE that you have identified
a passion, invest in yourself. Figure out what
you need to know, what kind of experience and
expertise you need to develop to do the things
that you feel in your heart you will enjoy and that
will sustain you both mentally and economically.

—MarthaStewart.com, c. 2019

MY DREAM, NOW in retrospect, then, was to be
an eclectic knowledge-gathering person in order
to be able to learn and then teach. I'm still doing
that.

—interview, Academy of Achievement, June 2, 1995

I WANT TO know a lot. I never stop reading, I
never stop investigating, I never stop asking
questions and trying new things.

—Bloomberg Breakaway CEO Summit, June 20, 2018

Focus on the positive. Stay in control, and never panic.

—*The Martha Rules,* October 11, 2005

I THINK MY biggest strength is my curiosity, and probably my biggest weakness is also my curiosity.

—*Next Question with Katie Couric* podcast, October 5, 2017

I AM A teacher. I think that my real value in this world is to be a really good teacher in the vast subject matter of "living."

—*The Henry Ford*, February 12, 2009

I WANT TO be remembered as a good woman who is a good teacher; one who is fun and has accomplished a lot.

—keynote address, Create & Cultivate conference, May 7, 2019

MY TWO MOTTOS that I always remind myself about: learn something new every day, no matter if you're so tired and you can't, you think you have to go to bed, learn something if you don't feel you have. Read something, look in a book, watch a movie that might inspire you. And the other thing is change. When you're through changing, you're through.

—commencement address at The Culinary Institute of America, April 15, 2011

I NEVER STOP making sure that what I say is the best of what could be said . . . If I planted a tree one way yesterday and somebody tells me of a better way to plant a tree, I think, you know, they're right, that's better. Then I change my way to accommodate.

—*Seventeen*, October 22, 2006

CHANGE IS GOOD—DON'T be afraid of it.

—*The Martha Blog*, August 29, 2019

WITHOUT AN OPEN-MINDED mind you can never be a great success . . . You can be directed and open-minded at the same time.

—interview, Academy of Achievement, June 2, 1995

I GET UP really early, and I go to bed really late. Sometimes I get tired, but it's not important. I have an exciting existence, and there's so much to do.

—MarthaStewart.com, c. 2019

[THE LAST THING I do before I go to bed is] probably set my alarm—well, my two alarms. I'm not afraid of not waking up; I'm just afraid of the clock not working or something.

—*W* Magazine, March 11, 2018

I CATNAP NOW and then, but I think while I nap, so it's not a waste of time.

—MarthaStewart.com, c. 2019

I don't like wasting time. I don't like not being productive.
I really want to maximize my time. Do as many things in a day as I can possibly do. That's how I live.
I just live like that.

—*The Henry Ford*, February 12, 2009

I'M NEVER SICK. Why get sick? It's a waste of time.

—*Nightline*, November 18, 2009

THREE RULES: NO whining, no kvetching, no complaining. They're all slightly different.

—*My Friends Call Me Johnny*, September 22, 2014

I LIKE TO know the way things are going to turn out. And I don't like surprises.

—*Vanity Fair*, August 2005

MY NUMBER ONE organizing principle? Give everything its own place; start there, and you will find the rest comes all the easier.

—*The Martha Manual: How to Do (Almost) Everything*, January 1, 2019

IF YOU HAVE a job, you do it well. That's been my obligation my entire life—do the job well.

—*The Oprah Winfrey Show*, October 5, 2010

I NEVER THOUGHT about what I wasn't good at. I was always willing to try anything.

—*Skimm'd from the Couch* podcast, December 5, 2018

SOMETIMES I SHAKE if I have to do something that I've never done before—maybe not noticeably, but inside. But I'll do it, because I know it's not an insurmountable task; I've done plenty of tasks in my life.

—*Martha Stewart Living* digital, November 2010

I DON'T THINK you should give credit to those people—those harsh critics. They're not worth it. I mean, they just shouldn't even be in my universe.

—*Vanity Fair*, September 2001

Without optimism, you're not going to make it. You're just not. I don't think you can acquire it. I've always been optimistic, and not fearful.

—*Vanity Fair*, August 2005

SUBSTANCE IS VERY important to me. Superficiality is not terribly important to me. Just showing something for the sake of showing it—say, a new pair of shoes or a derriere décolleté—is not necessarily the important thing to me.

—**BuzzFeed News, May 10, 2017**

WHEN I SEE grammar schools lightening courses to just the three Rs, that's very disappointing to me. It's cheating our youth by not offering them a way to express themselves. I don't think we, as a nation, can exist without creative input.

—***Martha Stewart Living* digital, November 2010**

I'M NOT AN extravagant liver. I live simply, personally. Although I do live on a farm of 150 acres.

—***Next Question with Katie Couric* podcast, October 5, 2017**

I NEVER LIKE to waste anything around the farm.
I always try to repurpose and reuse as much as
possible.

—The Martha Blog, May 1, 2019

I STILL DON'T really know what "bougie" is,
but it sounds like being bourgeois. And I don't
think that's so aspirational. I wouldn't want to be
bourgeois in any way. I want to be special.

—Kinfolk, September 5, 2017

I LOVE DOING laundry, I love cleaning the
basement. I even love ironing. I still have my
original Cuisinart, my original copper pots.
People need to know how to take care of these
things. Not everyone can pay people or find
people to do it for them. Do you realize how many
people put their good knives in the dishwasher?
It drives me bats!

—Sun-Sentinel, March 16, 1989

THE SUBJECT MATTER that I am really spending my time on has become an acceptable subject matter. Living, lifestyle, family, is now in the forefront of interest in America and I've just stuck with it. I mean, I've been doing this for years, and I never got angry, I never said, "You know, listen, I'm fighting for this subject." That wasn't my point. My point was to continue working in a subject matter knowing full well that finally it would be recognized as a viable subject once again.

—interview, Academy of Achievement, June 2, 1995

I'M VERY PROUD that I have really elevated the art of homemaking to an art form, rather than a drudgery.

—*The Henry Ford*, February 12, 2009

I HAD TO sacrifice a marriage because of the lure of the great job, the fabulous workplace. But, I don't regret it at all, because what I've done is something bigger and better than just one marriage. . . . People who are happily married, don't hate me for saying that. But for me, it's true. It's impossible for most of us to get that balance.

—CNNMoney, December 22, 2017

THERE ARE A few events that go on my calendar each year that I consider sacrosanct: my family's birthdays, my summer vacation in Maine, my Christmas party, my Easter egg hunt, and Trade Secrets. Almost nothing can cause me to miss these dates.

—MarthaStewart.com, April 27, 2015

I'm less mother than teacher. Hardly anybody I know thinks of me as a mother. Everybody loves their mothers, but not everybody likes their teachers. Teachers can be too hard on them. The love-hate stuff comes because of the teaching.

—*New York* Magazine, June 26, 2008

I FINALLY HAVE two grandchildren, who are two and three. Watching them, nurturing them, and paying attention to their development is very important to me. That's big on my list.

—interview, Intuit QuickBooks Connect conference, October 24, 2014

WHENEVER MY SCHEDULE allows, I always try to spend time with my dear grandchildren, Jude and Truman—we always have so much fun!

—*The Martha Blog*, June 28, 2017

MY DAUGHTER EMAILS me. When your daughter starts to email you instead of talk to you . . . It's horrible. You cannot forget human communication. When the Walkman first came out, I called it the Rudeman: Everybody who's listening to those is rude to me. I think part of the reason I got divorced was because of the Rudeman.

—*Wired*, July 24, 2007

COOKING IS NOT my favorite thing to do on the weekend, since I do it every day of the week. I enjoy my horseback rides, my gardening, my time with Jude and Truman, and socializing with friends.

—Reddit, March 6, 2014

I FEEL THAT I'm the same person that I've always been. I have grown and become, probably, smarter in my work and developed and built a business that's growing and growing and growing. But I'm basically the same person. My likes are the same. My tastes may have gotten a little better or a little bit more educated, but still, I always get up and clean out the kitty litter. I make sure everybody's home, all the animals. I go down through the garden and prune, and pick, and do all those things. I keep grounded. And by keeping grounded you can then see very clearly what's happened to you.

—interview, Academy of Achievement, June 2, 1995

THERE ARE SO many people in this country that are not cared for in any way, who just have nowhere to turn, nowhere to look. I'd like to make a difference in those lives.

—**Forbes 400 Summit, September 18, 2012**

WHENEVER MY BUSY schedule allows, I always try to attend benefit dinners that support good causes and important organizations.

—***The Martha Blog*, April 25, 2019**

THE MELDING OF cultures is really what I want to see happen in the United States and so does Snoop. There shouldn't be any divides. There shouldn't be any question that we can all get together and get along. There shouldn't be any discrimination.

—***The Hollywood Reporter*, June 8, 2018**

I DON'T READ novels very much because life is much better than any novel.

—**Bloomberg Breakaway CEO Summit, June 20, 2018**

WHEN YOU KNOW, inside, that you're good, that you've done well, and that you are an honest, good person, then you know that you can live through disaster.

—*Today*, **April 30, 2013**

IF YOU'RE GOOD, you'll always be good.

—*Dynamic Signal*, **2019**

THE ULTIMATE GOAL is to be an interesting, useful, wholesome person. If you're successful on top of that, then you're way ahead of everybody.

—*Seventeen,* **October 22, 2006**

YOU'RE AGING THE moment you're born. That's what aging is. It's just growing up. It's living. And as we get older, we get more powerful. Age is powerful.

—**SXSW music and media conference, March 11, 2019**

IT IS, INDEED, never too late to start a project, never too late to embark on a new career, never too late to realize a dream.

—*Living the Good Long Life: A Practical Guide to Caring for Yourself and Others*, April 23, 2013

Part II

GOOD THINGS

Food

SUSTENANCE IS FOUND in eating, of course, but it is found in cooking too.

—*Martha's American Food: A Celebration of Our Nation's Most Treasured Dishes, from Coast to Coast*, **April 24, 2012**

I'M SELF TAUGHT. I would love to go to cooking school. But I really, really, really am going to go work in a restaurant one of these days.

—**Martha Stewart YouTube channel, May 12, 2016**

I HAD JULIA Child's *Mastering the Art of French Cooking* in hand, and worked my way through from cover to cover.

—*Entertaining*, **October 27, 1998**

READING VOLUMINOUS AMOUNTS is very good for your curiosity and for inspiration. Talking to many, many different kinds of people, trying new kinds of things. I'm always trying new things. I'm always experimenting with the newest machines ... I also experiment with foodstuffs. I'm always looking for new kinds of food. I'm always looking at how to grow food better.

—interview, Intuit QuickBooks Connect conference, October 24, 2014

BAKING, YOU WILL find, as you indulge in this home art, offers comfort and joy and something tangible to taste and savor.

—*Martha Stewart's Baking Handbook*, November 1, 2005

I DON'T LIKE to have a meal without a dessert to end it.

—MarthaStewart.com, March 18, 2019

I LIKE EVERY kind of pie. I'm just a pie freak. I wrote the book *Pies and Tarts*, for heaven's sake!

—**Martha Stewart Facebook page, October 12, 2017**

I HAVE A golden rule for a pie crust: Make it cold. Bake it hot.

—*The Martha Stewart Show,* **July 25, 2013**

COOKIES, AFTER ALL, are wonderfully versatile things. Depending on how you mix, form, and bake a few simple ingredients, you can create cookies that make the perfect anytime snack, an elegant dessert, or a lunch-box treat.

—*Martha Stewart's Cookies: The Very Best Treats to Bake and to Share,* **March 11, 2008**

I DON'T THINK I've ever bought cookies in my life.

—**Reddit, March 6, 2014**

MY GUILTY PLEASURE is not at all interesting: it's a spoon of really good organic peanut butter, or a slice of American cheese from my housekeeper's drawer. I steal American slices sometimes—in the plastic, it's so horrible. But it's such a good snack.

—*Town & Country*, June 1, 2017

I TRY TO avoid plane food most of the time. I just don't find it very appetizing. And my hard-boiled eggs are just so much better than any eggs on the plane. They're from my own chickens. I take them for everybody I'm traveling with.

—*The New York Times*, October 11, 2017

I CANNOT EAT kimchi—it's too strong for me. I don't want to stink of garlic all day long . . . Beer is also fermented and wine is fermented and those are both perfectly good, too.

—*Kinfolk*, September 5, 2017

A homemade, home-baked, and handcrafted cake makes any occasion feel even more joyful, but you don't even need to wait for a special celebration to bake a cake.

—*The Cake Blog*, November 26, 2013

WHEN I'VE HAD a period of overindulging in rich foods, I don't diet; I never have. I don't believe in cutting out any food entirely, like butter, sugar, or cream.

—*Living the Good Long Life: A Practical Guide to Caring for Yourself and Others*, April 23, 2013

I DRINK GREEN juice every single morning that I make from things I grow.

—*Kinfolk*, September 5, 2017

EVERYBODY WANTS TO be able to pour the right wine. That's my motto: pour the right wine.

—*Late Night with Seth Meyers*, June 30, 2017

I LIKE COCKTAILS. I'm actually the cocktail mistress of the Martha & Snoop show. I make up all the cocktails and I feed them to Snoop, who's not really a drinker, so he gets totally drunk off of them.

—*Town & Country*, June 1, 2017

I LIVE THE food porn.

—*Kinfolk*, September 5, 2017

ONE TIP? HAVE all your ingredients assembled before you turn your oven on. And then don't forget to turn your oven on when you start to mix the ingredients together.

—Martha Stewart YouTube channel, May 12, 2016

I ALWAYS KEEP a bowl of coarse salt on hand for easy seasoning.

—*The Martha Blog*, September 18, 2007

I REALLY AM a believer in having gadgets that work, that are functional, and don't take up drawer space if they're only gonna be used once a year. Forget it—you don't need it if it's only once a year, unless it's something really extraordinary.

—Martha Stewart YouTube channel, August 16, 2016

I care just as much now about how things taste and look as I did years ago, but now I rely even more on freshness and goodness as the most important ingredients in my cooking.

—*Martha Stewart's Menus for Entertaining,*
October 25, 1994

OFTENTIMES THE OLDEST traditions, the antique varieties of fruits and vegetables, and timeworn techniques can still be the best.

—*Martha Stewart's Healthy Quick Cook*, October 28, 1997

THE RIGHT SAUCE can turn a plain dish into something extraordinary.

—*Martha Stewart's Grilling: 125+ Recipes for Gatherings Large and Small: A Cookbook*, March 26, 2019

I BRING IN a lot of stuff for the staff. I bring my own eggs in every week, hundreds of eggs from my chicken coops, so people are eating farm-fresh stuff all the time.

—*The Cut*, August 22, 2017

I HATE WHAT'S going on in the factory farms in America. And I cannot—I cannot abide the cruelty to the animals that we're being fed, the way grains are being grown. All of this gluten intolerance that's going on, it's a very serious problem. And why, why? When I was growing up, nobody was allergic to wheat. I didn't know one person with a peanut allergy. I don't think it's the peanuts and I don't think it's the wheat. I really think it's the processing. I think it's the way it's being grown, I think it's the way it's being sprayed, fertilized, all of that. And we have to really, really, as a country, pay attention to that.

—Talks at Google, November 6, 2011

COOK SEASONALLY, AND shop with an open mind. Don't go to the market determined to buy just the thing (and only the thing) that you plan to make. See what's fresh (and often, on special) and adjust your cooking plans accordingly.

—*Martha Stewart's Cooking School: Lessons and Recipes for the Home Cook: A Cookbook*, October 21, 2008

Entertaining

SHARING HAPPINESS AND goodwill and rites of passage are a serious part of living!

—Twitter, January 18, 2013

I CERTAINLY AM not of the "do it the exact same way: school of entertaining." I am an enthusiast for change, for subtly altering the traditional to make it more interesting, more creative, more inventive.

—*The Martha Blog*, November 29, 2011

THERE ARE AS many good formulas [for entertaining] as there are personalities. And invariably it is the evidence of a unique personality at work that makes an event special.

—*Entertaining*, October 27, 1998

1. Pay attention to your guests. 2. Interact with them. 3. Feed them fine food and wine.

—Reddit, March 6, 2014

WHEN I FIRST started entertaining, I inevitably invited too many guests and attempted dishes that were too elaborate, necessitating long periods of time in the kitchen... I quickly learned to be a participating hostess rather than a reclusive cook.

—*Entertaining*, October 27, 1998

THE CRITERIA FOR a "good thing" are complex, but straightforward. Is the project uncomplicated? Is it useful? Is it aesthetically pleasing? Is it something that many people will find interesting or pertinent to their lifestyle? Is it seasonal in nature? Are the materials used to complete the project easy to find? Is the result unusual?

—*Good Things: The Best of Martha Stewart Living*, April 29, 1997

ENTERTAINING FAMILY AND friends is always
challenging; setting a lovely table, always
fascinating.

> —*Martha's Entertaining: A Year of Celebrations*,
> **October 25, 2011**

NO ONE WILL know about your disasters if you
don't tell them.

> —*Entertaining*, **October 27, 1998**

EVEN IF YOU are just having a couple of friends
over for snacks and drinks, it pays to make a plan
and stick to it.

> —*Martha Stewart's Appetizers: 200 Recipes for Dips,*
> *Spreads, Snacks, Small Plates, and Other Delicious Hors*
> *d' Oeuvres, Plus 30 Cocktails: A Cookbook*, **September 8,**
> **2015**

So many people have forgotten but are rediscovering the satisfaction of planting a garden, decorating a house, planning a wedding, and finding them important forms of expression. The end result is liberating.

—*Weddings by Martha Stewart*, July 11, 1987

THE COCKTAIL PARTY is still my favorite way to entertain groups of friends, as well as one of my favorite catering assignments.

—*Martha Stewart's Hors d'Oeuvres: The Creation and Presentation of Fabulous Finger Food*, December 13, 1984

WOULD YOU LIKE to know a secret for entertaining? Here it is: a really good cocktail, carefully made with fresh ingredients and the highest-quality alcohol, served in a beautiful glass. This can set the mood for any party and get an evening off on the right foot.

—Richmond.com, July 12, 2014

SERVING BUFFET STYLE when hosting a big gathering is most practical and setting a beautiful and impressive buffet is easier than you think.

—NBC News, November 23, 2019

[IN ORDER TO entertain], have a good bar at home. It's very important to have the very best gin, vodka, scotch, bourbon, and tequila so you can make really, really good drinks. And with really good drinks, you can have a rich cheese and some really good biscuits as a snack. . . . When I entertain I like a very good drink and maybe some crudités or something.

—*Town & Country*, May 15, 2019

IN ASSEMBLING A plate, respect the integrity and the nature of each element: don't be haphazard, don't crowd, for the results are worth the extra few moments of time.

—*Entertaining*, October 27, 1998

I NEVER SERVE snacks at parties. It's either hors d'oeuvres or a meal. Hors d'oeuvres are prepared foods one would serve with meals or wine. Snacks are something you get out of a bag or a box.

—Reddit, March 6, 2014

IF YOU NOTICE a guest using the "wrong" fork, pick up the "right" fork and jam it into his head.

—"Martha Stewart's Worst Tips for Living," *Late Show with David Letterman*, 1995

INDULGE YOUR FANCIES: a love of Dixieland bands or baroque music, a fondness for peach ice cream or picnics or barbecues or the high-tea ceremony.

—*Weddings by Martha Stewart*, July 11, 1987

A WEDDING IS a microcosm of human affairs, the commercial and the ritualistic, the dreamy and the fashionable, but, in the end, it is a drama of two people, with all their ideas and fantasies, celebrating the continuum of life.

—*Weddings by Martha Stewart*, July 11, 1987

AT MY HOME, the kitchen is among the most important spaces. In fact, for many, the kitchen is the main hub—a place not just to cook, but also to work, relax, and entertain.

—*The Martha Blog*, September 19, 2016

I'VE ALWAYS LOVED Halloween. As a child, I enjoyed trick-or-treating and visiting homes decorated for the occasion, especially those that spooked and delighted young ghouls and goblins. As an adult, I still love to dress up—in the least, with a bit of special-effects makeup and tinted contact lenses. From costumes, to décor, to frightfully fun and tasty bites, my colleagues and I have always made the most of Halloween!

—*The Martha Blog*, October 24, 2018

EVERY YEAR I think that I will dine elsewhere on Thanksgiving Day—that for once I will not stuff myriad turkeys, crush pounds of cranberries, and burgee untold varieties of vegetables. Yet the tradition of the holiday is so much a part of what I do, what I live for, that to not cook and entertain on this day would seem tantamount to treason.

—*Martha Stewart's Menus for Entertaining*, October 25, 1994

EVERY YEAR BEFORE Thanksgiving, I send a general email to our employees, extending my very best wishes for a safe and lovely holiday. I also urge them to take photos of their table settings, their feasts, their families and their friends—I love seeing how others celebrate these special occasions

—*The Martha Blog*, November 29, 2016

Decorating

MY PASSION FOR exquisite linens began many years ago when my mother passed along to me a few beautifully embroidered hand towels and some pillowslips.

—*The Martha Blog*, December 28, 2011

I REALIZE NOW that I had moved to the country long before we actually left West 101st Street. Our apartment living room was crowded with huge country trestle tables, our kitchen tangled with herb plants, and I was raising orchids in our bathtub.

—*Entertaining*, October 27, 1998

EVERY HOME IS unique. Each one is a reflection of its era, its locale, and most significantly, the tastes and lifestyle of its occupants.

—*Martha Stewart's Homekeeping Handbook: The Essential Guide to Caring for Everything in Your Home*, October 31, 2006

THE HOMES I like the best are totally occupied, busy, and useful, whether it's a tiny little house or a great big one. Rarely do you find a great big house that's used in a good way. So I prefer smaller spaces that are full of books, full of things that people are doing.

—Wired, June 1, 2003

[MY BEDFORD KITCHEN] was brand new [in 2006] and I was so pleased to move in and use it. I am happy to say that the construction has held up extremely well . . . And because I chose such classic designs and soft, neutral shades, I haven't grown tired of the space.

—The Martha Blog, March 17, 2009

I LEARNED MANY years ago never to criticize, only compliment. Even if their home is horrifyingly awful.

—Reddit, March 6, 2014

Decorating is something one can learn to do ... it consists of the ability to turn a space, however small, into a home that is inviting, warm, and useful.

—How to Decorate: The Best of Martha Stewart Living,

June 1996

WHEN YOU SEE a pleasing form, take a few moments to let your imagination suggest a new function. Don't pass up a funky wrought-iron plant stand because it is old and rusty or you lack a green thumb. With one can of butter-yellow paint you can turn it into a charming bookshelf for a child's bedroom.

—*Good Things from Tag Sales & Flea Markets*, January 1, 2002

THERE ARE JARS in all the apothecary shops that I've been trying to find all morning. Now I'm running around looking for these jars. They're beautiful and they have leather which you wet and you draw over the top and it makes a very beautiful cover, a very inexpensive way to cover a jar. So you'll see that in my magazine soon because I think it's a real good thing, as I call 'em.

—interview, Academy of Achievement, June 2, 1995

I RARELY USE filler—which is baby's breath or sprays of other kind[s] of greenery like fern—in my arrangements. I like the flowers to speak for themselves.

—*W* Magazine, March 11, 2018

Gardening

ONE OF MY favorite pastimes is gardening. I am
a very serious gardener and am always thinking
about ways to improve the care and maintenance
of all my plants and trees.

—The Martha Blog, July 23, 2019

A GARDEN IS not just a place to grow things . . .
A garden is also a place where one can walk and
think, sit and contemplate. A garden should have
surprises, and should offer solace.

—Martha Stewart's Gardening: Month by Month,
October 12, 1992

I LEARNED THAT gardening was enjoyment
and sacrifice, that planting required inordinate
patience and fortitude, and that instant
gratification provided by planting large trees
and established plants could be tempered with
patience and smaller specimens, ultimately with
better results.

—Martha's Flowers: A Practical Guide to Growing,
Gathering, and Enjoying, February 27, 2018

To me, Good Things mean simple, practical solutions or tips that make everyday activities easier. The first time I used the expression publicly was later, on my television show. I was being filmed in the garden, and I held up my garden trowel, which had a brightly painted orange handle so it wouldn't get lost among the greenery. "It's a good thing," I said.

—*The Martha Rules*, October 11, 2005

ONE OF MY real joys in life, other than my family, pets, and job, is my greenhouse and all the plants growing in it.

—Fort Worth Star-Telegram, **January 20, 2018**

WHEN THE WEATHER is cold and uninviting, I love to visit my greenhouse and spend time with plants from warmer climates.

—The Martha Blog, **January 28, 2008**

I HAVE ALDERSON ginkgo from Alderson. I smuggled out some pods, and they are trees already.

—Vanity Fair, **August 2005**

IT'S NO SECRET how much I love planting trees and on Friday, I had a little dream come true. I planted a field of Christmas trees at my farm— 640 trees, to be exact!

—The Martha Blog, **April 20, 2009**

PLANNING A GARDEN is like being a painter and you want the results to be painterly.

—*The Martha Blog*, **November 24, 2010**

THAT'S A GREAT thing about gardening—if you're not happy with something, change it!

—*The Martha Blog*, **May 11, 2009**

I CARE VERY much about our environment, and am always seeking better ways to practice wholesome, organic gardening.

—*The Martha Blog*, **November 17, 2015**

I ALWAYS ENJOY learning about organic farms, stands and specialty markets—it is not only fun to see what others sell, but also very inspiring to learn how these entrepreneurs select their produce and promote sustainable farming practices.

—*The Martha Blog*, **February 20, 2019**

I PLANT LOTS of vegetables to share with family and friends, but I also grow them to use at the office whenever they're needed for magazine or television shoots.

—*The Martha Blog*, January 31, 2018

ONE OF THE most anticipated sights on the farm is my herbaceous peony garden in full bloom. No garden is complete without these beautiful plants, which are covered with large, imposing flowers in May and June. True perennials, herbaceous peonies can live for 100 years, becoming more impressive over time.

—*The Martha Blog*, May 9, 2019

I was always a very impatient person. I thought that by force of will I could get things done immediately; gardening has taught me patience. Nature, with her timetables, cannot be rushed.

—*Martha Stewart's Gardening: Month by Month,*
October 12, 1992

I LOVE COLLECTING seeds from favorite flowers to grow in next year's gardens. Seed saving is the practice of keeping seeds or other reproductive material from flowers, vegetables, grains, and herbs, for use from year to year. It's a rewarding pastime, a great way to save money, and the most economical way to produce new plants for the garden. It's also a nice way to share well-loved plants and flowers with family and friends.

—*The Martha Blog*, August 1, 2019

Animals

I HAVE ALWAYS prided myself on the good health and happiness of my pets.

—The Martha Blog, **October 23, 2009**

I HAVE, OH, hundreds and hundreds of pets. Including flocks of chickens, geese, I now have a, really, an ostentation of peacocks, I think I have 13 peacocks at present, I have six horses, I have three donkeys, I have 45 canaries, red canaries, I have 3 cats, and 4 dogs at present. And those are the pets I know about.

—Today, **May 28, 2019**

SHARING A HOME with any pet is a huge responsibility—one I never take lightly. It requires time, knowledge, and commitment to ensure every animal gets the best possible care. Once a month, I love to make my dogs a good supply of home-cooked food.

—The Martha Blog, **May 19, 2017**

It's always such a joy to see the animals at my farm growing and thriving— they are all so beautiful, curious and friendly.

—*The Martha Blog,* May 2, 2019

IT OCCURRED TO us at Martha Stewart Living that we had never really focused on the pleasures of raising backyard livestock. I developed my penchant for animal husbandry after I married and had a home of my own.

—*New York* **Magazine, June 26, 2008**

IT'S ALWAYS SO exciting when new chickens arrive at the farm. I've been raising chickens for a long time. Not only do I love keeping them for their fresh, delicious eggs, but I also enjoy their company and learning about their many different breeds and personalities.

—*The Martha Blog*, **June 22, 2019**

AT THE FARM, I currently have four coops that house more than 100 chickens.

—*The Martha Blog*, **March 21, 2015**

I TALK TO each of my pets in a special voice. I have a voice for my horses, I have a voice for my cats, I have a voice for my dogs. People think I'm crazy.

—*Today*, May 28, 2019

MY CANARIES LOVE to listen to classical music, which I keep on for them during the day.

—*The Martha Blog*, August 12, 2019

MY PETS ARE always there for me.

—*Today*, May 28, 2019

I THINK THAT you learn a lot from pets, and pets can certainly make you happier, can add a dimension to your household that even a child can't add. Because they're not really asking for anything.

—*Today*, May 28, 2019

Part III

HARD TIMES

Insider Trading Scandal

I was in the wrong place at the wrong time. I fell in a hole.

—*Fortune*, **November 14, 2005**

When I heard the verdict, I actually thought I was in a bad dream.

—*Late Show with David Letterman*, **2005**

I was less embarrassed than horrified, and that's a very different feeling. And horrified not only for me, but for everybody around me.

—*Late Show with David Letterman*, **2005**

What I did, was not against the rules.

—*20/20*, **November 7, 2003**

It's sort of the American way to go up and down the ladder, maybe several times in a lifetime. And I've had a real long up—along the way my heels being bitten at for various reasons, maybe perfectionism, or maybe exactitude, or something. And now I've had a long way down.

—*The New Yorker*, February 3, 2003

I SOLD MY remaining shares of ImClone not
because I had inside information, not because
I was secretly tipped, but because I set a price,
made a profit, and knew I could always invest
if I wanted to. To believe that I sold because
Sam was trying to sell is so very, very wrong. To
believe that I would sell, to avoid a loss of less
than $45,000, and thus jeopardize my life, my
career, and the well-being of hundreds of others,
my cherished colleagues and partners, is very,
very wrong.

—early version of letter to judge, *The New York Times*,
July 17, 2004

TODAY IS A shameful day. It's shameful for me,
and for my family, and for my beloved company.

—courthouse statement, July 16, 2004

I'M NOT AFRAID whatsoever. I'm just very, very sorry that it's come to this, that a small personal matter has been able to be blown out of all proportion, and with such venom and such gore, I mean it's just terrible.

—**courthouse statement, July 16, 2004**

PERHAPS, IN MY enthusiasm and in my quest for jobs well and quickly done I did not always take time to pat backs, or offer thanks for good work. I have been extra hard on myself and my work ethic and performance and I sometimes forgot that others need a bit more praise than I remembered to give. I am sorry for that and I wish I could always be polite, humble, respectful and patient.

—**letter to judge, July 15, 2004**

I SEEK THE opportunity to continue serving my community in a positive manner, to attempt to repair the damage that has been done and to get on with what I have always considered was a good, worthwhile and exemplary life.

—letter to judge, July 15, 2004

OF COURSE THAT is what it is all about. Bring 'em down a notch, to scare other people. If Martha can be sent to jail, think hard before you sell that stock.

—*Vanity Fair*, August 2005

MY PUBLIC IMAGE has been one of trustworthiness, of being a fine, fine editor, a fine purveyor of historic and contemporary information for the homemaker. My business is about homemaking. And that I have been turned into, or vilified openly as, something other than what I really am has been really confusing.

—*The New Yorker*, March 22, 2004

WE CALL IT 'the bus'—the wayward bus, getting hit by the bus. You know the 'D' things— death, dismemberment, dementia, disappearance, whatever they all are. All those 'D' things. It was something else. But I'm alive. There's the big difference.

—on MSLO contingency plans, *The New Yorker*, February 3, 2003

YOU CAN'T BE sorry for something that—let's see, how can I say this? I'm on appeal. You don't appeal if you think that you should be sorry. But I am sorry for the chaos, the damage, and the problems that the situation created. It hurt a lot of people. But I didn't hurt a lot of people.

—*Vanity Fair*, August 2005

MY PHILANTHROPY SUFFERED a grave setback when I was accused of a crime, and my personal fortune was greatly diminished by this problem that I faced. And all I could think of was how sad it was that being the focus of something, to me a very unfair focus, took away so much from what I could do to help others. Money is the best way to help in philanthropy. You can spend your time, you can do this, you can do that, but it all comes down, in the end, to how much money can be invested in a cause to make a difference.

—**Forbes 400 Summit, September 18, 2012**

I WASN'T EVEN accused of insider trading, but I don't want to get into that either. And one thing I do not ever want is to be identified, or I don't want that to be the major thing of my life. It's just not fair. But it's not a good experience, and it doesn't make you stronger. I was a strong person to start with, and thank heavens I was. And I can still hold my head up high and know that I'm fine.

—***Next Question with Katie Couric* podcast, October 5, 2017**

FIVE MONTHS IS a long time in a company, and ultimately it's a tiny percentage of my life, if you really think about it. If [going to Alderson] had happened earlier in my life, it would have been worse, because it would have killed what I was doing. It hurt what I was doing, but it didn't kill it, and I am very grateful for that.

—*Vanity Fair*, August 2005

Prison and Home Confinement

LUCKILY, TIME FLIES for me. I know that other people have fallen apart. I could have fallen apart.

—*Vanity Fair*, August 2005

I HAD A legal problem that no one could foresee, and no one could anticipate, and I didn't do anything wrong . . . I'm not talking about it now because it's still such a weird situation. But I had to go to jail for 5 months, and it kind of bothered me a lot. But I survived it very nicely, because I said, "Don't let it get you down," and "You're better than this."

—*Skimm'd from the Couch* podcast, December 5, 2018

I ASKED MY fellow inmates a couple months later, I said, "How did I behave that first day?" Because everybody was watching me. They said I was walking around in a daze. I smiled at everybody, said hi to everybody.

—*Late Show with David Letterman*, 2005

IT'S UP TO each and every person [at Alderson] to maintain the family ties, to maintain the friendships, to maintain connection with the outside, to maintain knowledge of what's going on around them in the world. Because it is a tiny little place, in a tiny little spot, in a tiny little speck of the universe, and nobody cares, once you're there. So you have to care.

—*Vanity Fair*, August 2005

THEY SAID YOU could do one ceramic every three months or something [in prison], but I sort of persuaded them that the entire nativity crèche was one project.

—*The Oprah Winfrey Show*, October 5, 2010

I think many of us have an inner strength that you do not know until you are tested. [Prison] was a test. I kept my head up. I kept my friends intact, most of them. I kept my spirit high, and I moved on.

—*The Oprah Winfrey Show*, October 5, 2010

LET'S GET TO the reason I'm here tonight, which is to give Justin Bieber some tips to use when he inevitably ends up in prison. I've been in lockup and you wouldn't last a week so pay attention. The first thing you'll need is a shank. I made mine out of a pintail comb and a pack of gum.

—"Roast of Justin Bieber," March 30, 2015

YOU WOULD NOT want to eat that food. That's why I made jam out of the crabapples on the trees.

—on prison food, Cannes Lions International Festival of Creativity, June 23, 2016

IT WOULD HAVE been great to tell them that I'm a vegetarian.

—on prison food, *Fortune*, November 14, 2005

I FOUND OUT that I could really exist with pretty much nothing.

—*Late Show with David Letterman*, 2005

I HATE LOCKDOWN. It's hideous.

—*Vanity Fair*, August 2005

HOME DETENTION . . . is designed to be
confining. You're not supposed to be doing any
business when you are in jail, and when you go
away, things happen. Now when I go back—for
the few hours a week I can—I am running around
to do every single thing I can.

—*Vanity Fair*, August 2005

AT ALDERSON, I could go out every morning
at 6:30 a.m. and be back only for one count at
4 p.m., and then out until 10 p.m. every night.
On 100 acres. Here I can't. And 48 hours is very
confining. I think those kinds of regulations
should be really looked at by the regulators.

—on post-prison house confinement, *Vanity Fair*,
August 2005

I CAN'T GO out until 10:30 p.m., but I can sit on the porch, as long as I don't go past the footprint of the house.

—on post-prison house confinement, *Vanity Fair*,
August 2005

I ALMOST PLANTED [daffodils] on the outside of that wall, but at the last minute I switched the plan and put them on the inside, and thank God. If I hadn't I wouldn't have been able to see them, because I could not go around to the other side of the wall. It's hard. It takes a kind of strength to get through it, because it's very confining. And I'll never get used to the ankle bracelet. No matter what they say, you don't get used to it, because it hurts.

—on post-prison house confinement, *Vanity Fair*,
August 2005

I OVERCAME A very difficult, nasty situation. I
also had a very supportive daughter, I also had a
supportive family, and I had for the most part, a
supportive company. And the best of all, I had an
extremely supportive audience.

—interview, **Intuit QuickBooks Connect conference,**
October 22, 2014

EVERYBODY TELLS YOU "Oh, whatever happens
to you it'll make you stronger." F-U-C-K them.
It's so mean. That is the stupidest thing because
it doesn't make you better at all, and it could ruin
you.

—interview, **Intuit QuickBooks Connect conference,**
October 22, 2014

THAT YOU CAN make lemons out of lemonade, and what hurts you makes you stronger—no, none of those adages fit at all. It's a horrible experience. Nothing is good about it. Nothing . . . Especially when one does not feel one deserves such a thing.

—*Next Question with Katie Couric* **podcast, October 5, 2017**

I DON'T HAVE a long memory for bad things, so I'm trying very hard to put it out of my mind and get on with the future.

—*Late Show with David Letterman*, **2005**

I HAVE LEARNED that I really cannot be destroyed.

—*Fortune*, **November 14, 2005**

Part IV

EMPIRE

Business Philosophy

LOOK FOR OPPORTUNITIES around you and start with your own expertise, whether it's your vocation or avocation. Stick with it. Don't give up. Defend your ideas, but be flexible. Success seldom comes in exactly the form you imagine it will.

—*The Cut*, August 22, 2017

WHEN I'M ASKED how and when I knew I would build a very strong and influential brand, I always say that it just "happened." It happened, but not without years of hard work and dedication, not without constant retooling of my peculiar and intense self-education in all things that pique my curiosity, and not without complete immersion in the idea of home and the vast subject of what I call "living."

—*The Palladium-Item*, January 8, 2017

IT'S ALL ABOUT having ideas, having energy to make those ideas into something, and having the wherewithal, whether it be personal, or borrowed, or education, to build something of lasting value.

—*Next Question with Katie Couric* podcast, October 5, 2017

I'VE ALWAYS LOOKED for a void. And I still am looking for a void in everything I do.

—*Skimm'd from the Couch* podcast, December 5, 2018

I TOLD [MY audience] to find an idea that appeals to a broad audience, and to find what doesn't exist that you love that you have in your mind that can fill that void that everybody wants. Need and want and void—those three words are very important in business.

—*The Martha Blog*, August 29, 2019

BEING SINCERE ABOUT what you do, and what you learn, and what you can teach is extremely important.

—commencement address at The Culinary Institute of
America, April 15, 2011

SCOUTING IS A term we use for gaining inspiration, and ideas, we always scout when we go anywhere—it's fun and invaluable for a creative co.

—Twitter, April 5, 2013

YOU SEARCH FOR inspiration and develop the best. The few things that make it to the masses—that is the success of the brand.

—*Vanity Fair*, August 2005

I REALLY BELIEVE we can do anything we set our minds to. Sometimes that's a struggle; it's harder than it should be, and I think I have paid my dues.

—*O, The Oprah Magazine*, August 15, 2000

EVER SINCE I started Martha Stewart Living, I've said there's no job too big or too small for me to do. So if the jar of honey has to be filled, I'll fill it, but I'll also scrub the numbers. I wanted to make creativity equal to business, and I relish the fact that many of my editors and art directors became very competent in business.

—*Martha Stewart Living* digital, **November 2010**

I GET HUNDREDS of emails a day. The phone used to ring hundreds of times, but now it's email. Nobody has access to my email. I do all my own emails.

—*The Cut*, **August 22, 2017**

LONG-TERM PLANNING HAS never been my forte—like many people, I am more creative and productive with a sense of immediacy.

—*Holidays: The Best of Martha Stewart Living*,
September 20, 1994

I have always found it extremely difficult to differentiate between what others might consider my life and my business. For me they are inextricably intertwined.

—*The Martha Rules*, October 11, 2005

I HAVE PROVEN that being a perfectionist can be profitable and admirable when creating content across the board: in television, books, newspapers, radio, videos.

—*O, The Oprah Magazine*, August 15, 2000

I CAN ALMOST bend steel with my mind. . . . I can make myself do almost anything. But you can get too strong like that, so you have to be careful. You have to temper your strength.

—*O, The Oprah Magazine*, August 15, 2000

I MANAGE IT all—I woman it!

—*Into the Gloss*, March 16, 2015

I THINK BAKING cookies is equal to Queen Victoria running an empire. There's no difference in how seriously you take the job, how seriously you approach your whole life.

—*O, The Oprah Magazine*, August 15, 2000

I think you have to be really, intensely serious about your work, but not so serious that you can't see the lightness that it may also involve. You have to have that lightness too. You have to not be so heavy-handed and so ostentatious. It's very important not to be.

—interview, Academy of Achievement, June 2, 1995

No OTHER WOMAN has created this kind of business in such a short time, from scratch, from, you know, baking cookies in the basement. That's really fun.

—**CBS News, November 22, 1999**

My LIFE IS my business, and my business is my life.

—**CNN, July 19, 2004**

WHEN WORK IS based in passion, it does not feel like work—it feels fulfilling and empowering.

—*The Martha Rules*, **October 11, 2005**

CHOOSE YOUR EMPLOYEES wisely. Get the very best like-minded people you can and some that are even smarter than you are. Don't ever be afraid of that. I think that having smart people around you—in my business it has to be smart and creative—those are the people that you really, really want to have around you as you grow, as you thrive.

—**Bloomberg Breakaway CEO Summit, June 20, 2018**

IF YOU ARE really going to be hiring these people, they have to be good. So I am trying to get across my business precepts: (1) People matter. (2) Invest to get perfection. (3) You have to take risks.

—*Vanity Fair*, **August 2005**

IT IS TRULY gratifying that so many extraordinarily talented people have started and grown their careers at my company.

—*The Martha Blog*, **January 27, 2011**

IF SOMEBODY COMES to me looking for a job, I'm not going to be mean to them. They're trying. It's a wonderful opportunity to show people that I actually have good advice to give to young entrepreneurs, and business lessons to teach.

—*Vanity Fair*, August 2005

I PROMISE YOU, if they were paying for this with their own money, they would know how much it costs per day. Find out. It's called management. M-G-T. It's important.

—on managing people and products, *Vanity Fair*, August 2005

THIS FRUGALITY IS deeply embedded in the culture of my company. It is how I have always run my businesses, and in large part why they have been profitable. It is not about being cheap but being frugal.

—*The Martha Rules*, October 11, 2005

One of the most important things we can do in America right now is encourage creative entrepreneurs and small business owners to grow and thrive, create new jobs and support our economy. And I'm proud to be part of that.

—keynote speech, American Made Awards, November 7, 2014

TO SAVE ON transportation costs, we have our own shuttle service, which runs hourly.

—on MSLO having locations in two parts of Manhattan, *The Martha Blog,* July 31, 2008

I HAVE SOMETIMES probably forgotten, and I know I have, forgotten to pat the back of someone, or said, thank you, you know, enough times, or even maybe once sometimes. So I—you know, I wish I were perfect. I wish I were just, you know, the nicest, nicest, nicest person on Earth. But I'm a businessperson in addition to a creator of domestic arts. And it's an odd combination. No excuse. But if I were a man, you know, no one would say I was arrogant.

—CNN, July 19, 2004

I WOULD NEVER say, 'You're fired,' so we are trying to come up with other ways to say it. For instance, if someone is from Idaho, I could say, 'You're back in Boise for apple-picking time.'

—*Vanity Fair,* August 2005

I LIKE TO teach, as do the other people here at Martha Stewart Living. We want to teach you the best recipes, the best techniques—we bring in experts who also are fantastic teachers.

—**Martha Stewart Facebook page, July 3, 2018**

IT'S VERY HARD to take sides openly, especially in a media business. I can't do anything very overt, and I feel bad about that, because I get requests every single day to be overt in my feelings. And you can't, because 50% of your readership is on this side and 50% of your readership is on [that] side. I have a magazine and an obligation to my employees to pay attention, so it's very hard to be political. A lot of our entrepreneurial leaders, like the Elon Musks, they take sides and they get into trouble, and you just can't. If you're running a big corporation, it's better to run your corporation, pay attention to the everyday workings of your company, of your employees, and focus on that.

—**Bloomberg Breakaway CEO Summit, June 20, 2018**

Knowing your passion, working hard to keep it alive, enjoying it every minute of every day, even when the going gets difficult—these are the hallmarks of an entrepreneurial expertise that you build and develop and maintain and evolve.

—*The Martha Rules*, October 11, 2005

BEING AN ENTREPRENEUR is not easy, but it is exciting, fun, and amazingly interesting and challenging . . . It requires eyes in the back of one's head; constant learning; curiosity; unflagging energy; good health, or at least a strong constitution to ward off illness; and even the strength and desire to put up with sleep deprivation and long hours of intense concentration.

—*The Martha Rules*, October 11, 2005

ANYBODY WITH AN entrepreneurial bent has a real fine and exciting chance to do something new and different. And it takes a tremendous amount of hard work, it takes a tremendous amount of perseverance to take your idea to the first level, the next level, the final level—if there ever is one. You don't ever want to meet the final level you want to keep going, because it's an exciting process.

—Bloomberg Breakaway CEO Summit, June 20, 2018

I ADMIRE THE courage and self-reliance it takes to start your own business and make it succeed.

—Interview, **October 16, 2013**

Media

I THOUGHT, IF I don't write a book, my grandchildren, if I ever have any, will never know what grandma did in her life, because catering is so ephemeral. You do it, it's gone . . . So I wanted to make sure I recorded my ideas, the beautiful recipes.

—*Next Question with Katie Couric* podcast, October 5, 2017

I STARTED TO write books because I started to realize my friends were just like me—we all needed some encouragement to entertain better, we needed better recipes that could be done that weren't too complicated. And there were, at that time, 1982, very few illustrated cookbooks . . . And I considered myself kind of a really good cook at the time, so I wrote this book *Entertaining*.

—*Next Question with Katie Couric* podcast, October 5, 2017

I PUBLISHED MY first book, *Entertaining*, finding a niche that needed filling and providing my audience with facts and ideas and recipes I knew they wanted and needed. Why? Because I was that woman—I needed what I was offering.

—**YMA Fashion Scholarship Fund's Annual Awards Gala speech, January 10, 2019**

I WROTE MY first book in 1982. Titled *Entertaining*, it expressed, as well as I could then, my very intense thoughts about planning and preparing and giving parties of all types—large or small, lavish or simple. I am pleased to say that over the years my philosophy and sentiments have remained the same.

—*Great Parties: The Best of Martha Stewart Living*, **November 11, 1997**

My books are 'dream' books to look at, but they're very practical. People can take the recipes, the ideas, and use them every day, because what I'm giving them is not a fantasy, but a reality that looks like a fantasy.

—*Entrepreneur Magazine*, October 10, 2008

I WRITE THIS beautiful book, and it was a big hit, and I think that that irritated a lot of people— irritated them to death, because they felt that I hadn't paid my dues. And I also think that they looked at that book and probably said, 'Boy, why didn't I write this book?'

—on writing her first book, *Entertaining*, *Vanity Fair*, September 2001

I FOUND OUT, rightly or wrongly, that once you write a book that's acknowledged as a good book, you are an expert.

—interview, Intuit QuickBooks Connect conference, October 22, 2014

I'M ALWAYS WRITING from my own viewpoint; that's very, very important to me. I wouldn't do a book any other way. It's what makes my books successful. Yet ironically, it's the very thing they are criticized for.

—*Sun-Sentinel*, March 16, 1989

BOOK SIGNING EVENTS are a wonderful way to
meet the people who love my products and my
publications. I always get very helpful feedback
from customers.

—*The Martha Blog*, January 17, 2018

I HAVE SIGNED tens of thousands of books over
the years—and I always like to use a colored
pen that best coordinates with the colors of the
book—it is a detail that is very important to me.

—*The Martha Blog*, May 16, 2019

BY 1990, I was a 49-year-old mother of a grown
daughter, a divorcee, and I knew I was onto
something big. I've been dubbed a "late bloomer,"
and I love the moniker. I published the first issue
of *Martha Stewart Living* that year, and have
been pursuing my dreams ever since.

—*Fort Worth Star-Telegram*, January 3, 2017

WHEN I WAS doing my proposal for the magazine with Time Warner, I remember meeting with the big honchos and I showed them a prototype for a July issue, and July, of course, includes July 4th. They said, this is all great, but what the heck are you going to do next year? Because they thought it was finished! I said, I think we can probably not repeat ourselves for 20 or 30 years with all the ideas. It's about having creative teams, about making up new ideas, making up new ways to celebrate traditional things. And that's what we do all the time.

—**Talks at Google, November 6, 2011**

IT SEEMS LIKE yesterday that we published our very first issue of *Martha Stewart Living*. Each and every one of our 260 issues has been true to my original vision that a true lifestyle publication must instruct, inspire, and enhance the reader's life in as many ways as possible.

—**MarthaStewart.com, November 9, 2015**

I WAS THE audience. I was the housewife, with
child, with home, with garden, in the suburbs.
I and millions of other women needed exactly
what I was going to do in that magazine.

—on *Martha Stewart Living*, *Next Question with Katie
Couric* podcast, October 5, 2017

IT'S ALL ABOUT the product, and I'm the face of
the product, the founder of the product . . . I sold
a lot of magazines—other people's magazines—by
being on the cover, and many, many newspapers.
To me, it was horrible.

—*Vanity Fair*, August 2005

I, AS THE founder of Martha Stewart Living Omnimedia, was inducted into the ASME Magazine Editors Hall of Fame. It is really such a thrill to receive an award for a vision of mine that I, and my staff, have been living and believing since the very first issue of *Martha Stewart Living* magazine in 1991. I applaud all of those who have worked with me and have made this vision a reality.

—*The Martha Blog*, January 30, 2009

MARTHA STEWART LIVING has expanded to Thailand, Indonesia, and Korea.... This all started from my traveling abroad and meeting many people who love our magazines and wanted them where they live.

—*The Martha Blog*, December 22, 2010

ONE THING I just love about putting together my television show is meeting all of the talented and fascinating guests that appear each day. I learn so much from them, as I hope you do too.

—*The Martha Blog*, **March 27, 2008**

I'M SO PROUD we've built such a strong bond with our viewers. They can trust our shows to give them quality information in a beautiful way. I love to know that I empower cooks in all 50 states to be the bakers and chefs they want to be.

—**speech, General Managers of Public Broadcast Service meeting, May, 2014**

IT IS ALWAYS so much fun appearing on television shows, where I can share information, and teach something new to those in the audience, and to those watching at home.

—*The Martha Blog*, **March 20, 2017**

28 YEARS OF television! Once I got some grease on me, but we just ignored it. But I've never had to have two of everything. Many, many people on TV have two outfits the same. I have never done that. It's just a waste. Plus I don't wear aprons. I used to wear aprons, but I don't wear aprons anymore. I just don't care about aprons.

—**Martha Stewart Facebook page, October 12, 2017**

WHEN I STARTED my business, the internet was a baby, but I had a computer. I learned how to use that computer. I learned how to write and use the internet to do research, to do all of the things. Now social media is another challenge for all of us. How do we maneuver and negotiate social media to make a difference without wasting a tremendous amount of time doing so?

—*Next Question with Katie Couric* **podcast, October 5, 2017**

MY BLOG IS an instructional tool that's a very serious, well written, beautifully photographed, sort of like a magazine series that goes on and on and on and on. It's a lot of stuff that we don't put in the magazine because we don't have enough pages to include what I put in my blog.

—*W* Magazine, March 11, 2018

I DO BLOG every day and I like doing my blog because I try to write and photograph an educational blog that will actually inspire people to take a little time away from the computer. Maybe they can read it early in the morning when they get up and go out and plant a tree or raise some chickens or collect some eggs or do something. I do think that we have to find balance in this technological age.

—interview, Intuit QuickBooks Connect conference, October 22, 2014

Authenticity is extremely important in all social media.

—The Martha Blog, June 18, 2010

DAVID CAAR OF *The New York Times* interviewed me about my use of Twitter. We were talking about me having just surpassed 600,000 followers on Twitter. I explained that it took me 2 years to reach 600,000 subscribers with *Martha Stewart Living* and only a fraction of that time on Twitter.

—The Martha Blog, May 15, 2009

I FIRST STARTED with books, and if you can sell 500,000 copies, you're doing really well. A magazine has four or five times that number of readers. The television did the rest.

—New York Magazine, May 15, 1995

ONE DAY I'M presenting Maya Angelou with a Living Legend award and then I fly off to Miami and attend a Victoria's Secret fashion show. And then yesterday, the multi-platinum rap artist, Snoop Dogg, appeared on my television show and taught me some of his very own language called Snoop-guistics.

—The Martha Blog, November 19, 2008

I LIKE HIS laid-back energy—I like his outspokenness, I like his sense of timing, and I really enjoy to watch him cook. He's so particular, his little tiny bits of this and that, and it all finally comes together.

—on Snoop, MarthaStewart.com, April 2, 2019

IT REALLY IS fun. I call it a melding of cultures. I mean, here's Compton and Nutley.

—on *Martha & Snoop's Potluck Dinner Party, Next Question with Katie Couric* podcast, October 5, 2017

[SNOOP] LIVES ON a compound—like my compound, I guess, but his is full of people, where mine is full of plants and animals.

—*Kinfolk*, September 5, 2017

[I'M] A LITTLE bit more complicated in my recipe selection than Snoop. . . . He likes to eat but he has . . . um . . . he has very specific tastes. And he's not so keen on trying new things if they're not familiar.

—Kinfolk, **September 5, 2017**

I LIKE SNOOP because he is put off by so many ingredients. And he's scared of things and that's fun, too—it's fun to shock him.

—Today, **September 21, 2018**

I GET KIND of high from secondary smoke. I'm not a smoker myself, but the smoke is quite thick around the set.

—Hollywood Reporter, **June 8, 2018**

OUR DEMOGRAPHIC IS very broad now especially with the Snoop Dogg show. From teenagers to people in their 70s.

—ABS-CBN News, **August 20, 2019**

I try to live the life I teach to the hundred million or so users and viewers and readers of the stuff that we create. And it's essential, I think, to live a life like that if you're going to teach that kind of life.

—interview at Chicago Ideas Week, October 20, 2015

WHEN I WALK down the street now, every truck driver knows who I am. If I go through Harlem, every single guy on the street corner knows who I am.

—Hollywood Reporter, June 8, 2018

MY STAFF AND I had created a large and growing library of real content—photographs, recipes, craft ideas, gardening advice, decorating tips, collecting information—all of "evergreen" value with a huge potential for synergy with other media platforms, such as television, radio, books, and newspaper columns. If we could combine all of those elements into one omnimedia company, the whole of that would certainly be greater than the sum of its parts. This was not just about owning a business; it was about building a brand. I understood that we had our Big Idea.

—The Martha Rules, October 11, 2005

MARTHA STEWART LIVING Omnimedia is an innovative media company and our strategy has always been to be where ever our consumers are—in print, on TV, on the web, and at retail stores.

—*The Martha Blog*, December 14, 2010

I HAD WORKED really hard to build a superb company, Martha Stewart Omnimedia. And it was kind of a cutting edge company. This was a company that actually took into consideration the Internet, the television, the printed word, the media, as well as merchandising. So it was really truly omnimedia, and we still are.

—*Next Question with Katie Couric* podcast, October 5, 2017

I STARTED A magazine, I wrote books, I started a television show that kind of reiterated but also expanded upon the kinds of things that were covered in the magazine. I found out that Living and Lifestyle is a limitless subject matter.

—*How Success Happens* podcast, February 28, 2018

Merchandising

WE ALWAYS SAY that media leads and we started off, of course, writing books first, then the magazine, then television and radio, then product. So media leads and merchandising follows. You build up an interest, you build up a curiosity in your readership and a desire for things, and then the merchandising follows.

—**Bloomberg Breakaway CEO Summit, June 20, 2018**

EVEN THOUGH WE were giving people the how-to ideas, many people wanted the product, so it was a perfect way to expand into product development. We continue to do products in many different categories.

—**keynote address, Create & Cultivate conference, May 7, 2019**

WE, AT MSLO, have a strong understanding of what people can live without and what people cannot live without. We know that the consumer wants high quality at the best value and, as a company, that is what we strive to offer.

—*The Martha Blog*, **April 15, 2009**

I WANTED TO see how the Martha Stewart Craft line was looking and to inquire how it was selling. I certainly wasn't disappointed. The display was neat and tidy, as was the entire store and Jeanne, the Assistant Manager, informed me that sales were brisk.

—on an unannounced visit to a Michael's™ crafts store, *The Martha Blog*, July 23, 2008

I REALLY ENJOY these visits because I love meeting all the sales associates and hear their feedback on our line.

—on surprise trips to Home Depot stores to see the Martha Stewart Living products, *The Martha Blog*, July 15, 2011

I'VE ALWAYS LOVED kitchens and the central role they play in our daily lives with family and friends. Over the years, I've designed many kitchens for my homes and have learned so much in the process. So when I was given the opportunity to design my own line of kitchens exclusively for The Home Depot, I already had years of experience and inspiration to draw from.

—*The Martha Blog*, September 15, 2014

EVERYBODY WHO SHOPS at Kmart, and there's about 77 million people a month shopping there, they want beautiful things. And I'm trying to get really gorgeous things into the store.

—*Late Night with David Letterman*, June 6, 1989

We have a very large audience—they trust our taste, and love our products and colors, and that's what we're trying to continue to appeal to. High-quality products at an affordable price point, made available to all consumers: That's what's core to our brand DNA.

—*Architectural Digest*, **March 19, 2019**

THE BEST QUALITY you can get at mass market is what we sell at Kmart. And the next level up is Macy's. And that's what we're doing with Macy's, is yet another price level of goods for the department store shopper. So some people shop department stores, some people shop the Kmart, Sears, and that's what we are providing to both of them.

—"Ask Martha" video, c. 2018

AND AGAIN I applied my democratic approach to this unique form of design—clothes have to be well-made, they have to fit, they have to serve a purpose, they have to feel good and they have to last . . . And above all, they have to be beautiful.

—on her QVC fashion line, YMA Fashion Scholarship Fund's Annual Awards Gala speech, January 10, 2019

I AM DELIGHTED to establish this partnership with Canopy Growth and share with them the knowledge I have gained after years of experience in the subject of living. I'm especially looking forward to our first collaboration together, which will offer sensible products for people's beloved pets.

—on CBD products for pets, *Canopy Growth*, February 28, 2019

AT MSLO, DESPITE my brief absence, we managed to plan and execute many exciting and wonderful new things—from my new television show in front of a live audience to *The Apprentice: Martha Stewart.* Great furniture was designed; houses created; a newly acquired magazine, *Body+Soul,* was beautifully redesigned; and we planned the content for a 24-hour-a day, 7-day-a-week satellite radio program on the Sirius radio station. Would we have done all these things were we not forced to step back and reevaluate who we were and where we wanted to go? Possibly not.

—*The Martha Rules*, October 11, 2005

THERE'S STILL PLACES in the world that I
haven't been that I do want to go. And making
sure that the brand that I have built, the Martha
Stewart brand that I have built, has a good, long,
strong life.... I want to make sure that it has a
good future. I think all of us businesspeople ...
want to make sure that what we're creating, what
we're building, has longevity and value, and value
to others, not just oneself.

—interview, Intuit QuickBooks Connect conference,
October 22, 2014

Milestones

1941

- Martha Helen Kostyra is born to Polish-Catholic immigrants Martha Kostyra (aka Big Martha), a schoolteacher, and Edward Kostyra, a pharmaceuticals salesman, in Jersey City, New Jersey.

- The second of six children born to the Kostyras, Stewart grows up in the working-class suburb of Nutley, New Jersey. Her modest upbringing, along with her mother's passion for cooking and sewing and father's passion for gardening, lays the foundation for her wide range of skills. Her father's strict perfectionism and self-sufficiency is imbued in Stewart as well.

- As a high schooler, she babysits the children of baseball legends Mickey Mantle and Yogi Berra. Stewart organizes parties for neighborhood children and those she babysits, demonstrating her interest in party planning from a young age.

1956

- Stewart begins her modeling career at the age of 15. She walks in fashion shows and is featured in TV and print ads for brands such as Breck, Clairol, Unilever, and Tareyton cigarettes.

1959

- After earning good grades while also working and participating in extracurricular activities including the school paper and Art Club, Stewart graduates high school. She inscribes in her high school yearbook: "I do what I please, and I do it with ease." Partial scholarship in hand, she heads to Barnard College in New York City.

1961

- *Glamour* magazine names Stewart one of America's "10 best-dressed college students."

- Stewart marries Andrew (Andy) Stewart, a Yale law student. For the wedding, she wears a dress that she and her mother made together. The couple honeymoon in Vermont and travel extensively across Europe as newlyweds.

1964

- Stewart graduates from Barnard College with a bachelor's degree in history and architectural history. She continues to model as her husband establishes his law practice.

1965

- In September, she gives birth to a daughter, Alexis.

- The Stewarts purchase a rundown 19th-century schoolhouse in Middlefield, Massachusetts, and renovate it.

1967

- Inspired by her stockbroker father-in-law, Stewart begins working on Wall Street as a stockbroker with the small firm Monness, Horstman, Williams, and Sidel. She soon earns a six-figure salary and gains valuable insight that will later serve her well as an entrepreneur.

1971

- The Stewarts move to the historic farmhouse Turkey Hill in Westport, Connecticut. In later years, Stewart buys the surrounding four acres and adds a barn.

- She renovates the home, including stenciling the living room floor by hand. She begins teaching cooking classes out of the house and undertakes occasional catering jobs.

1973

- Stewart ends her career as a stockbroker. Jobless for the first time since early high school, Stewart earns her real estate license and starts to regularly cater events from her kitchen.

- By planting a garden at Turkey Hill, Stewart is able to cultivate vegetables and fruits for meals. She will expand her garden over the next few years to a size that can sustain her family throughout the year. Later, she will plant enough to also share produce with many of her employees.

1976

- Stewart starts a catering business called Uncatered Affair, with her friend Norma Collier in Westport, CT. They host dinner parties and cooking classes as well as cook for events. The company is a success, and she begins earning a reputation for carefully curated dinners and themed décor.

- She turns her daughter's outgrown playhouse into a chicken coop and begins raising chickens on her farm. This eventually expands into a full farm of Friesian horses, Sicilian miniature donkeys, Black Welsh Mountain sheep, peacocks, ducks, geese, and more.

- Collier and Stewart part ways, and Stewart begins selling pies and homemade food items out of The Common Market, a food court in an upscale shopping mall. This new business venture quickly becomes a storefront called The Market Basket. She continues catering events on the side.

- *People* magazine features a story on Stewart and her husband and mentions her prestigious clients, including Paul Newman.

- Stewart is hired as a food editor for *House Beautiful*. She is also asked to write occasional columns for *The New York Times*. Her reputation as an expert in homemaking and entertaining grows.

1977

- On the first day of the year, Stewart incorporates herself and her food writing, catering, and other

cooking and baking ventures under one name: Martha
Stewart, Inc.

1979

- Stewart secures a $25,000 advance from Crown
  Publishing to write her first book.
- Stewart's father, Edward, dies.

1982

- *Entertaining*, Stewart's first book, becomes a
  bestseller, selling over 625,000 copies. Prior to
  publication, Stewart and her publisher clashed over
  the appearance of the book. While Crown wanted to
  include only a few, black and white photos, Stewart
  successfully argued that the book's purpose was
  immersion and thus required many color photos to
  be beautiful and distinct. She embarks on a national
  book tour.

1984

- Her book *Hors d'Oeuvres* is published.

1986

- Stewart appears on a public television special,
  Holiday Entertaining with Martha Stewart. Newsweek
  magazine notes her shaky standing with other food
  professionals, as she is accused of practicing "the art
  of showing off" and has no formal training.

1987

- Stewart and Andy separate. Stewart says that she had to sacrifice her relationship to succeed in her career. She says she was rarely home once her work started gaining traction, and when she was home, she was planning catering events and not spending time with her husband and daughter. Andy describes it differently, citing her verbal abuse and poor treatment of him as the reason he left.

- Kmart appoints Stewart as their "lifestyle consultant." They initially use her in advertisements and publicity work, but soon develop a line of affordable, Martha-branded merchandise, including tableware and bed sheets, with her input.

1990

- Time Warner partners with Stewart to publish *Martha Stewart Living* after she pitches the trailblazing concept of a magazine focused on entertaining. Stewart serves as editor-in-chief and appears on the cover of each edition.

- Stewart and Andy divorce. Andy obtains a court order to prevent Stewart from discussing their relationship with the press and becomes involved with, and later marries, Stewart's much-younger former assistant, Robyn Fairclough.

1991

- Stewart signs a 10-year deal with Time Warner for *Martha Stewart Living* and spin-off television shows and books, as well as regular appearances on *The Today Show*. She agrees to appear on various daytime programming without pay in exchange for free advertising for the magazine and her merchandise.

- Stewart goes on a book tour for *Martha Stewart Gardening Month by Month*.

1993

- Stewart climbs Mount Kilimanjaro, where she meets her future business partner, Sharon Patrick.

- The TV program *Martha Stewart Living* debuts. The 30-minute weekly show is based on the magazine and is nationally syndicated. In the first episode, Stewart explains the difference between jam and jelly and details the process of composting. The program is soon expanded to a full hour.

1994

- The magazine *Martha Stewart Weddings* launches.

- Tom Connor and Jim Downey publish a parody magazine called, "Is Martha Stuart Living?". The 64-page issue includes innovative homemaking processes like making water from scratch, stenciling the driveway, and using a protractor, T-square, and 12,000-watt professional heat gun to construct precise hospital corners. Its bestseller status inspires two sequels, "Martha Stuart's Better Than You at Entertaining" and "Martha Stuart's Excruciatingly Perfect Weddings."

1995

- Stewart begins writing "Ask Martha," a nationally syndicated newspaper column. At its peak, the column is featured in almost 250 papers and reaches millions of readers weekly.

- Stewart wins the first of many Daytime Emmy awards for her TV show, *Martha Stewart Living*.

- For an episode of her TV show, Stewart visits the White House and hangs a homemade wreath with First Lady Hillary Clinton. Once the cameras stop rolling, Stewart packs up and takes the wreath with her.

- "Martha by Mail," an insert in *Martha Stewart Living* magazine, launches. It becomes a separate, direct mail catalogue due to its success.

1995

- Julia Child, Stewart's idol, guest stars on her TV show.

1996

- *Saturday Night Live* airs "Martha Stewart Topless Christmas," a sketch starring Ana Gasteyer as Stewart.

- Stewart joins the Revlon board of directors.

- Kevin Sharkley joins Stewart's media and merchandising business. Sharkley will go on to be executive design director and executive vice president of Stewart's empire, the only person to be listed as co-author on a Stewart book, and the only individual other than Stewart to be featured on a cover of *Martha Stewart Living* magazine.

1997

- Martha Stewart Everyday, an exclusive line of bed, bath, and paint home goods, is launched at Kmart; the line continues to be sold at Kmart until 2009.

- Stewart, assisted by Sharon Patrick, buys her publishing, television, and retail franchises and merges them to create Martha Stewart Living Omnimedia (MSLO). To obtain ownership of her magazine and TV show, Stewart reportedly pays Time Warner $75 million. This decision to merge her interests to become a "force for the 21st century" receives favorable media coverage. Her business accomplishments begin to overshadow criticisms of her strict personality and perfectionism. She is lauded as the perfect hostess and the "definitive American woman of our time."

1998

- Kmart's Martha Stewart Everyday line expands to include kitchen textiles and window treatments.

1999

- MSLO trades publicly. With an opening price of $18 and closing price of $35, the initial public offering of MSLO is hugely successful. This briefly makes Stewart a billionaire, the first self-made female billionaire in the United States.

2000

- MSLO reports profits of $21 million and annual sales of $285 million. Stewart is included on *Forbes'* list of America's 400 wealthiest people.

- Kmart adds the Martha Stewart Everyday Kitchen collection.

2001

- Stewart sells 4,000 shares of ImClone Systems stock one day before the FDA announces that one of the company's cancer drugs would not be reviewed. According to Stewart, the sale is due to outstanding instructions she gave to her broker, not because of information she received illegally. ImClone's stock price tumbles with the FDA announcement, and the sale saves Stewart about $40,000.

- Kmart's Martha Stewart Everyday brand generates about $1.5 billion in sales.

2002

- Kmart files for bankruptcy protection. Stewart states she'll stick with the retailer.

- Stewart is nominated to be a member of the New York Stock Exchange board. She is approved to serve a two-year term.

- *Martha Stewart Living* circulation reaches 2 million copies per issue.

- As the Securities and Exchange Commission (SEC) and Justice Department investigate Stewart for the timing of her sale of ImClone shares, she and her lawyer state she had no inside knowledge of the FDA's decision, but fail to mention whether she knew her friend Sam Waksal, the CEO of ImClone, and his family were trying to sell shares. Stewart maintains she told her broker to sell if the shares dipped below $60, and predicts the investigation will be resolved shortly. Once her broker's assistant pleads guilty to receiving money and valuables in order to keep quiet regarding the circumstances surrounding Stewart's stock sale, Stewart relinquishes her position on the board of directors of the New York Stock Exchange. MSLO reports a 42 percent drop in third quarter earnings, and predicts a severe drop in fourth-quarter earnings as well.

- The website Savemartha.com launches to support Stewart and counter negative publicity about her. It sells Save Martha! merchandise including hats, t-shirts, and beach coolers.

2003

- In June, Stewart is indicted by a federal grand jury on nine counts of securities fraud, obstruction of justice, and conspiracy, related to her sale of the

ImClone stock. She pleads not guilty. The Securities and Exchange Commission files a civil suit for insider trading, wishing to bar her from running public companies. Stewart steps down as chairman and CEO of MSLO, but remains chief creative officer and creates a new position, founding editorial director, which allows her to continue to run the company in everything but name.

- *Everyday Food* magazine launches. This is the first MSLO magazine that does not carry Stewart's name.

- MSLO launches a furniture line with Bernhardt.

- *Martha, Inc.*, a made-for-TV movie about Stewart's historic rise and fall, airs. It stars Cybill Shepherd as Stewart and focuses most of its time on the insider trading scandal.

2004

- Stewart maintains her innocence and does not testify at her trial. She is convicted of conspiracy, obstruction of justice, and lying to investigators— charges that can net 20 years in prison. She receives a five-month sentence that she unsuccessfully appeals, and then, for certainty's sake, decides to serve her sentence and file subsequent appeals later. Stewart requests imprisonment at one of two locations: Danbury, Connecticut or Coleman, Florida, citing these locations as easiest to visit for her family and attorneys. Instead, she is sent to Alderson Federal Prison Camp in West Virginia, beginning in October. Alderson is likely chosen due to its remoteness and inaccessibility to the media.

- Shares of MSLO jump after Stewart's sentencing.

- Viacom drops *Martha Stewart Living* from the CBS and UPN networks.

- Stewart resigns from Revlon's board of directors. She also resigns as chief creative officer of Martha Stewart Living Omnimedia.

- MSLO announces that *Martha Stewart Living* will go on hiatus for the twelfth season (2004-2005). It will not return to air.

- *Body + Soul* magazine is acquired by MSLO.

2005

- During her prison term, Stewart's net worth triples to over $1 billion as MSLO shares continue to soar.

- In March, upon release from Alderson, Stewart begins to serve five months of home confinement. She is allowed to leave her home for 48 hours a week for work, religious services, food shopping, and doctor's appointments, and must wear an electronic ankle monitor at all times. Her home confinement is extended by three weeks for undisclosed reasons. This period is followed by two years of probation.

- Another TV movie about Stewart, *Martha Behind Bars*, broadcasts, again starring Cybill Shepherd as Stewart.

- *Martha Stewart Living* receives three Emmy nominations, despite being on hiatus.

- *Time* magazine honors Stewart at a dinner as one of their "100 Most Influential People," sparking debate as to whether she is in violation of her house arrest for attending the celebration. Her publicist contends the appearance is business-related.

- Stewart begins hosting a daytime TV talk show called *The Martha Stewart Show* (or just *Martha*).

- PBS debuts the TV program *Everyday Food*, after the flagship magazine. Senior members of MLSO's editorial staff host the show, focusing on easily adjustable 30-minute recipes for supermarket shoppers and everyday cooks.

- The TV show *The Apprentice: Martha Stewart*, a spin-off of *The Apprentice*, airs. Her daughter serves as a boardroom consultant. It runs for one season. Donald Trump, the host of the original show, blames Stewart for his own declining ratings, though they had been falling prior to Stewart's original airdate. Stewart responds in turn that she was supposed to have "fired" Trump in her first episode, with her show poised as successor, not a spin-off, to his.

- *Martha Stewart Weddings* wins a National Magazine Award for General Excellence (250,000 to 500,000 circulation). The award, also known as the Ellie, honors publications that are editorially excellent, technically innovative, and imaginative.

- *The Martha Rules: 10 Essentials for Achieving Success As You Start, Build, or Manage A Business,* publishes. The book includes Stewart's personal anecdotes and suggestions for success, and is inspired by encounters with fellow prisoners at Alderson who looked to her for advice on how to start their own businesses.

- Sirius Satellite Radio launches *Martha Stewart Living Radio* channel. The weekly call-in show allows Stewart's listeners to ask her questions about entertaining and home-related problems.

2006

- MSLO and KB Homes collaborate to build a townhome community in Cary, North Carolina. The townhomes are designed to be affordable yet elegant, and are inspired by the exteriors of Stewart's homes in New York, Connecticut, and Maine. Each townhome has four individual units with unique floor plans, and is merchandised with Stewart-branded products.

- Stewart appears as herself on the Thanksgiving episode of the TV show *Ugly Betty*.

- *Fortune* names Stewart one of the 50 most powerful women in business.

- The U.S. Court of Appeals confirms Stewart's conviction will not be overturned. Stewart pays $195,000 as part of a settlement with the SEC for the insider-trading probe. Her sale of 4,000 shares of ImClone stock saved her $40,000, making the sale much more expensive than the initial loss would have been, especially if one includes the costs of the court cases, appeals, and the loss of reputation and business for MSLO. As part of the agreement, she cannot serve as the CEO or CFO of any public company for five years.

2007

- Stewart's mother, nicknamed Big Martha, dies at age 93. Before her death, she made many appearances on Stewart's television programs.

- Stewart founds the Martha Stewart Center for Living at Mount Sinai Medical Center, focusing on the health care needs of older adults. The center is a handicap-accessible, one-stop shop for primary and outpatient care for the elderly, and also provides yoga, nutrition planning, music therapy, and fall-prevention programs. Stewart's focus on elder care is spurred by the aging baby boomer population and a lack of health care professionals equipped for dealing with geriatric and palliative issues.

- Macy's begins exclusively selling a new line of Martha Stewart-branded products and home goods.

- Michaels releases the Martha Stewart Crafts line, including a special Halloween collection of thematic decorations, invitations, embellishments, and food packaging supplies.

- E&J Gallo Winery produces Martha Stewart Vintage wine. The initial release of 15,000 cases includes Sonoma County Chardonnay, Cabernet Sauvignon, and Merlot.

2008

- The book *Martha Stewart's Cooking School* debuts as a *New York Times* bestseller.

- Walmart stores release Stewart-branded craft items under two new lines: Martha Stewart Celebrate and Martha Stewart Create. The Celebrate line includes ready-made, paper-based wedding essentials including cake toppers and invitation stationary. The Create line includes crafting and scrapbooking supplies such as paper, appliques, and cutting mats, as well as pre-packaged activity kits.

- Stewart is denied a visa to enter the United Kingdom, likely due to her conviction for lying to government agencies in the United States. Other individuals who have been denied entry to the UK include radical Islamic preacher Yusuf al-Qaradawi and rap star Snoop Dogg.

- MLSO acquires the Emeril Lagasse brand.

2009

- Kmart and Martha Stewart Living end their partnership. MSLO signs deals with Home Depot and PetSmart.

2010

- Home Depot launches Stewart-branded products in an effort to appeal to female and more design-oriented consumers. Products include closet organizers, décor items, outdoor furniture sets, and paint.

- Hallmark and Stewart announce television partnership. The Hallmark channel runs Martha

Stewart programming eight hours a day, five days a week.

2011

- Stewart becomes a first-time grandmother when her daughter Alexis has a baby daughter, Jude. Grandson Truman follows in 2012.

- The TV show *Martha Bakes* airs on PBS.

- Stewart is inducted into the New Jersey Hall of Fame. Prior inductees include Thomas Edison, Frank Sinatra, Toni Morrison, and Harriet Tubman.

- Stewart reassumes a position on the board of directors of MSLO, as soon as she's legally allowed.

- J.C. Penney and MSLO form a 10-year deal featuring Stewart's home décor products.

- Stewart's daughter, Alexis, releases the book *Whateverland: Learning to Live Here*, with her friend and radio co-host Jennifer Hutt. She is heavily critical of Stewart's parenting style. Stewart brushes off the comments, calling the book "hilarious and enlightening."

2012

- Macy's sues MSLO for breach of contract for entering into a deal with J.C. Penney, claiming it was in violation of their exclusive rights to Stewart-branded kitchen, bed, and bath products.

- Staples features a new line of Stewart's office supplies.

- Stewart hosts another PBS show, *Martha Stewart's Cooking School*.

- Stewart's chow chow, Ghenghis Khan, wins Best in Breed at the Westminster Dog Show.

- Stewart introduces a new MSLO effort: the American Made Awards and Summit. American Made is an annual symposium that honors and highlights 10 up-and-coming, innovative, determined, and creative American entrepreneurs in the fields of agriculture, manufacturing, design, and style. The symposium returns annually until 2016.

2013

- Appearing in New York State Supreme Court, Stewart defends her deal with J.C. Penney. But the result is that because of the breadth of Stewart-designed and branded products available at Macy's, J.C. Penny is barred from featuring her kitchen, bed, and bath products. This leads the retailer to scale back its partnership with MSLO.

2014

- Stewart's sister, Laura Plimpton, dies at age 59. Plimpton worked for Stewart and MSLO for more than 25 years.

- *Martha Stewart's Cooking School* wins the James Beard Award for Outstanding Television Program, In-Studio or Location. The James Beard Awards are considered the "food Oscars" with journalism, broadcast, book, and restaurant categories.

- Macy's and MSLO reach an undisclosed settlement and continue their partnership.
- Stewart's Twitter followers surpass 3 million, largely due to her photos of dishes she cooks and eats and her amusing comments about aspects of modern life (like drones—they are "controversial but fabulous").

2015

- Stewart makes a splash with her X-rated roasting of Justin Bieber on Comedy Central. This marks a stark change in popular perception, away from her public image as cold and fairly humorless. This new approach allows Stewart more freedom in her communications with the press and public and accords her a host of new, young fans.

- Stewart launches a chain of coffee shops called Martha Stewart Café. The cafés are distinguished by their Martha-esque simple white countertops with pops of red, tidy displays, and elements of black calligraphy.

- Sequential Brands purchases Martha Stewart Living Omnimedia for $355M. The purchase includes all of MSLO's holdings. Stewart remains chief creative officer and sits on the board of directors.

2016

- The home meal-kit delivery service Martha & Marley Spoon is introduced. Meal options include a full Thanksgiving dinner.

- Stewart appears as herself in the movie *Bad Moms*.

- Stewart and Snoop Dogg team up to create the TV show *Martha and Snoop's Potluck Dinner Party* on VH1. The two formed a friendship in 2008 when Snoop appeared on an episode of *Martha*. On *Potluck*, they host celebrity guests and share recipes. Her fan base expands accordingly. The show is nominated for eight Emmys as well as an MTV Movie + TV award the following year. Stewart credits the show and her friendship with Snoop as influential to her understanding of the world.

2017

- Stewart partners with QVC to develop skincare, fashion, and food and beverage lines. The multi-platform retailer advertises new Stewart products ranging from copper bird feeders to faux leather dog vests.

- A photo on Instagram of Stewart flipping off a portrait of Donald Trump while simultaneously giving a peace sign to an adjoining painting of her friend Snoop appears. This is one of the few times Stewart publicly expresses strong political opinions.

2018

- Stewart serves as a recurring judge on the TV cooking show *Chopped*. Her first episode is themed around "million-dollar meals" with a variety of high-end ingredients for contestants to use, including gold leaf and camel-milk chocolate.

- Stewart documents her first Uber ride on Instagram. She photographs the messy interior of "the most expensive version" with complaints of cancelled pickups and navigation issues. The next year, Stewart partners with Uber to promote their Uber Black relaunch.

- *Martha's Flowers* is published. Stewart and her close friend and employee Kevin Sharkey co-authored the gardening and flower arrangement compendium. This is the only book on which Stewart has shared authoring credit. Some believe this is a sign that Sharkey will eventually inherit Stewart's empire.

2019

- Four years after purchase, MSLO owner Sequential sells MSLO and all of its holdings to Marquee Brands for $175M. Sequential takes a $193M loss on the sale, accounting for inflation.

- MSC Cruises and Stewart partner to develop culinary itineraries for shore excursions, with meals and experiences curated by Stewart. The cruise ships' dining rooms and restaurant will feature meals by Stewart.

- Stewart receives the YMA Fashion Scholarship Fund's Lifetime Achievement Award for her lifelong effort to share her knowledge of handmade, homemade, innovative, practical, beautiful, and "good" things, along with her more recent forays into fashion design.

- Partnering with Canadian marijuana producer Canopy Growth, Stewart begins developing a line of CBD pet products. Her goal is to increase well-being and reduce anxiety in household and barnyard animals.

- Stewart reveals she is working on her first autobiography, and plans to make it her 100th book.

2020

- Stewart is announced as the 2020 inductee to the Licensing International Hall of Fame. Past inductees include George Lucas, Charles Schulz, and Walt Disney.

- Continuing a long-standing feud with Goop founder Gwyneth Paltrow, Stewart slams a newly released Goop product, the $75 vagina-scented candle, saying, "it's a lot of guys who are horny" that make the product successful, rather than a discerning, wellness-focused clientele.

- Food Network TV launches *Bakeaway Camp With Martha Stewart*, in which home bakers vie to win challenges in order to obtain prizes including personal cooking lessons with Stewart and a kitchen worth $25,000.

Acknowledgments

I want to thank Kelsey Dame, Kristina Dehlin, and Katie Aiello-Jones for their invaluable contributions to the preparation of this manuscript.